Biggest, Most Awesome Machines Ever!

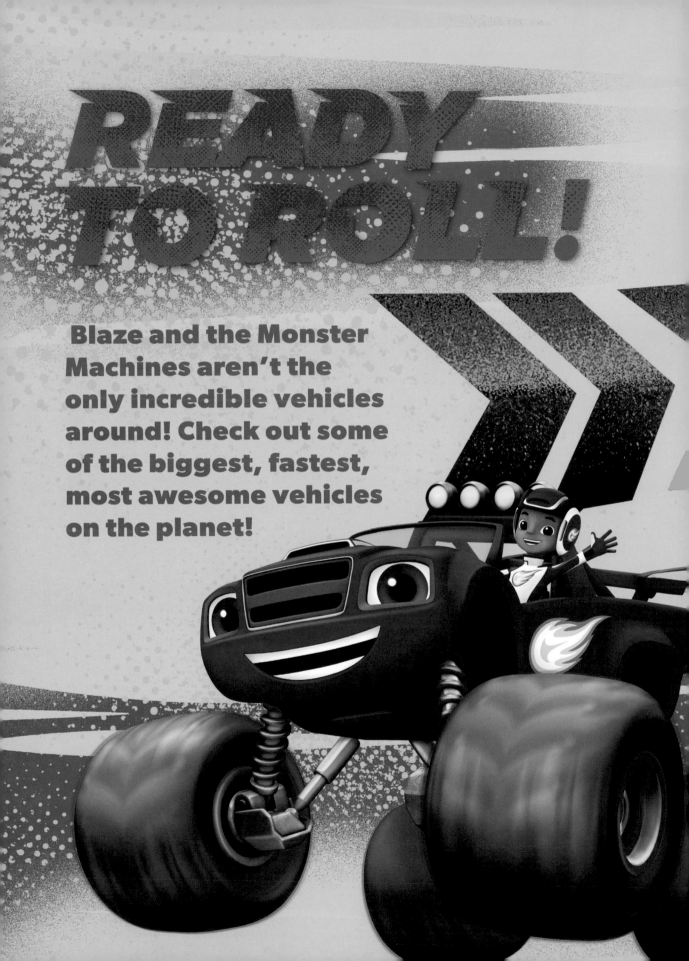

READY TO ROLL!

Blaze and the Monster Machines aren't the only incredible vehicles around! Check out some of the biggest, fastest, most awesome vehicles on the planet!

TABLE OF CONTENTS

MONSTER TRUCK

In 1986, a man named Bob Chandler built the biggest monster truck ever. Since then, no one's been able to make a bigger one! Named **Big Foot 5**, this monster truck is 15 feet, 6 inches tall—that's taller than a female giraffe!

DID YOU KNOW?

MASS is a measure of all the stuff that makes something heavy. This truck can use its big size to smash, bash and crash!

Zeg like!

5

TRACTOR

Tractors are used for pushing or pulling farm equipment. The biggest farm tractors use hydraulics for extra power!

DID YOU KNOW?

HYDRAULICS make machines really strong. Hydraulics move fluids from one place to another and that gives machines a lot of power!

Yeehaw! I could use a powerful tractor with hydraulics on my farm!

7

SCHOOL BUS

A jet-powered school bus is sure to get kids fired up for school! This hot ride shoots flames and can reach 367 mph! But don't expect to get a ride on this bus. It was built for demonstrations—it needs an engine so big, it only fits 3 people inside!

I could totally beat Blaze if I were jet-powered!

DID YOU KNOW?

All vehicles use **ACCELERATION!** Whenever you're going one speed, and then you start going faster, that's acceleration!

I don't know, Crusher, Blaze is pretty fast!

JEEP

The world's largest Jeep is four times the size of a regular one! It weighs a whopping 4.4 tons. Regular-sized Jeeps are pretty awesome, too! They have tires with deep treads that allow them to drive just about anywhere, from rocky terrain to sandy beaches to the jungle!

DID YOU KNOW?

When something has good grip, it's getting *traction*!

Jeeps have
great grip,
just like me!

119 JTB

11

ROLLER COASTER

Kingda Ka is the tallest rollercoaster in the whole world. This wild ride is 456 feet tall—that's the same height as 75 refrigerators stacked on top of one another! It's also the fastest roller coaster in the USA!

That coaster has some crazy velocity! Velocity is how fast you're going in a certain direction.

DID YOU KNOW?

This roller coaster is about the same height as the Great Pyramid of Giza!

FIGHTER JETS

Fighter jets are planes with excellent *maneuverability*! That means they can be controlled much more easily than regular airplanes. Their pilots can make them do barrel rolls, loops, fly upside down and more!

DID YOU KNOW?

The world's fastest manned jet airplane flew more than 2,000 mph!

I love
aerial
tricks!

15

BLIMP

The world's largest blimp is called the Airlander 10! A blimp's shape is very aerodynamic so it can move through the air easily.

DID YOU KNOW?

Blimps stay in the air because they're filled with helium! Helium is a gas that's lighter than air, which makes it float.

Air flows around the blimp's smooth shape! That's what makes it aerodynamic.

17

JET PACK

The fastest jet pack ride in the world was piloted by a man named Eric Scott. Scott went 68 mph in a hydrogen peroxide-powered jet pack!

DID YOU KNOW?

When something is pushed forward, that's *propulsion*. Jet packs are propelled by either gas or water!

That little pack is mini and mighty—just like me!

ROCKET SHIP

Saturn V was a rocket that took people to the moon. Saturn V is taller than the Statue of Liberty! It's the biggest rocket NASA ever built, but they're working on an even bigger one!

Let's go to the moon!

DID YOU KNOW?

NASA's first rocket went to space in 1950!

AMPHIBIAN

Amphibians are vehicles that can go straight from land to water. A lot of them look like boats with wheels, but some look like regular sports cars—until you see them speeding across the water!

DID YOU KNOW?

Amphibians are named after animals that live in water and on land, like frogs, toads, and salamanders!

Those machines are ready for anything!

CRUISE SHIP

MS *Harmony of the Seas* is the world's largest cruise ship! It has 20 restaurants, 4 swimming pools, an ice rink and a whole lot more. It even has a waterslide that's 10 stories tall!

DID YOU KNOW?

BUOYANCY is the ability of an object to float. Ships float, so they have buoyancy, unlike anchors, which sink!

Hubcaps, that's a big boat!

You said it, Blaze!

SUBMARINE

Nicknamed "Golden Fish," the K-222 was the fastest submarine in the world! It had a crew of 82 people. That's a big crew!

DID YOU KNOW?

The more **MASS** something has, the more energy it takes to move it!

All that mass reminds me of you, Zeg!

Zeg like
submarine!

HOVERCRAFT

Because hovercrafts glide by pushing air straight down, they can only be driven on flat surfaces such as grass or water. If the terrain isn't smooth, everyone is in for a rocky ride!

DID YOU KNOW?

When a hovercraft gets going, it builds up a lot of **MOMENTUM**. *Momentum* is a measure of the strength of a moving thing.

That hovercraft is so fast—just like Blaze!

29

ALL THOSE MACHINES WERE
BORN TO PERFORM!
WHEN IT COMES TO AMAZING
VEHICLES, THERE ARE NO LIMITS!

And that's
how it's done!

Media Lab Books
For inquiries, call 646-838-6637

Copyright 2017 Topix Media Lab

Published by Topix Media Lab
14 Wall Street, Suite 4B
New York, NY 10005

Printed in China

ISBN-10: 1-942556-75-6
ISBN-13: 978-1-942556-75-6